90 Day Author

How to become THE authority in your local market
as a published author

NINA HERSHBERGER

Printed in the United States of America

Easy Read Publishers
11650 Olio Road
Suite 1000-329
Fishers, IN 46037

"It does sometimes 'take a village'. In the part of my life as a career, professional, direct-response copywriter, I often live with fear and trepidation about what will become of my copy once headed over to the clients, to then be 'produced' for both online and offline media. It's vital to have somebody converting it to promotional books, booklets, shock 'n awe packages, illustrated sales letters, etc. who is NOT an 'artist' and who DOES understand direct-response. Such birds are rare. Nina Hershberger is just such a rare bird. She can be trusted. She has produced countless media tools and packages consistent with 'Kennedy-style' over many years. She also has a good portfolio of proprietary, plug-n-play marketing media ready for clients' use. It's always a sigh of relief, good news when I hear that the client is working with Nina."

DAN S. KENNEDY, Direct Marketing Strategist & Copywriter, author of the No B.S. book series as well as THE ULTIMATE SALES LETTER, available on Amazon

TABLE OF CONTENTS

Competing in the "New Economy"

A s a business owner, you likely find yourself facing increasing and continuous competition. What used to be only a game of tug-of-war with another local competitor or two is now the day of the "big box" store, online marketers, and others who have altered the entire business landscape. Many times these competitors enter with superior capital and other resources. They move into your territory, often with terrifying aggression.

If this is happening to you, you might think your only options are
    * compete on price

* add gimmicks to your business, or
* just plain give up.

Your business has always survived on local presence, relationships, and "doing a good job." Now with technology, global conglomerates, and a shifting economy, new opponents can do it so much faster and cheaper that it seems almost impossible to keep up.

And yet...

You're confident that customers who buy from you LOVE you

You provide a great product or service for a fair price.

But perhaps you just can't seem to attract enough new customers to keep your company thriving or growing the way you want.

In this age of phones that double as computers, tablets that deliver your newspaper, TV, and radio, and cars that know when your tires need air, many business owners think that technology alone is the answer. They think it will give them the edge they need over their competition.

But face it: you can spend thousands of dollars to design, create, and implement technology enhancements...only to find that by the time you roll them out, they're almost obsolete. You've stayed even, but not gotten ahead. So you know technology alone is not the answer.

What if there were a better way?

One that was subtle yet effective.

One that was able to convey your story and to let your prospects know why you are the best choice for them without them feeling SOLD.

I'm here to tell you that there is.

I call it the **expert phenomenon.**

The quickest way to tap into this phenomenon - to become a perceived "expert authority" - is to write a book

I build long-term relationships in my business by providing marketing solutions to my clients that yield tangible results.

My methods deliver

- measurable profits,

- long-term customers/clients/patients,

- and a repeatable, dependable, predictable way to create real growth and opportunity.

  Head and shoulders above marketing techniques is to write a book. My marketing mentor says:

  "*You MUST write multiple books for your business and use them in your marketing*"

Books are not leading-edge technology; much the opposite. Yet the businesses who use it as a lead-generating tool have seen not only increased profits but transformation in their businesses

With the "expert phenomenon" on your side, customers not only don't run; they seek you out to request your services or your products. Why? Because you are the expert.

Once you have your book, it will become a tool that opens doors you thought could never open.

It will turn cold prospects into hot leads.

Clients will stop asking, "How much?" and start asking, "How soon?" (And the even better news is…you can start charging more for your product or service.)

Read on to find out how you can put the "expert phenomenon" to work for you!

Nina Hershberger

574-320-2522

Here I am with Dan in the basement of his house during my 2 days spent with him privately.

My First Book

Several years ago, I witnessed the positive effect publishing a book had on a competitor's business. It made me want to write my own book — to build my professional credibility. The problem was I had never written a book, and I wasn't sure where to start.

I started doing research on just how you go about writing, editing, and printing a book. It seemed overwhelming at first. I had a thriving coaching and consulting business and didn't really have the time to take on such a huge task.

Then I was approached about the idea of a co-authored book: for $3,000, I could get a chapter published in a book with the famous marketer on the cover.

I thought it was a great idea!

The celebrity of this marketer would attach to me, and I would be viewed as an expert by association. And writing one chapter would be much easier than writing a whole book.

I wrote and submitted my chapter. After months of waiting, I finally got my book shipment. But when I opened the box, my excitement turned to disappointment.

Although I was part of the book, my name wasn't on the cover.

My chapter was in the book, but so were 34 other people's chapters!

I realized I was just "another chapter in the book," when I really wanted it to be about ME.

I wanted my name on the cover; I wanted my bio on the back. I wanted my chapter first. I got none of that for my $3,000.

But out of those lemons came lemonade

Shortly after that I made a proposal to 5 business owners I was coaching to submit their best marketing ideas and I would put them together in a book.

- Each owner would get to "license" the contents of the book,

- With their name and custom title on the cover,

- And I would give them 20 printed books for them (with the ability to buy more at a wholesale price)_ — all for $3,000.

They agreed.

It turned out to be a much bigger task than I had anticipated. Having a consistent "voice" was very important, and getting the book to sound like it was written by one person meant major rewrites.

But when the books arrived, it was worth it

Here is my copy of "our" book, along with the covers of all the others in our "writers' group".
My version of the book.

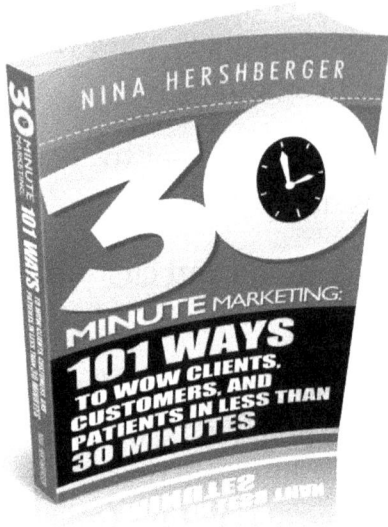

Still a GREAT book and available on Amazon.

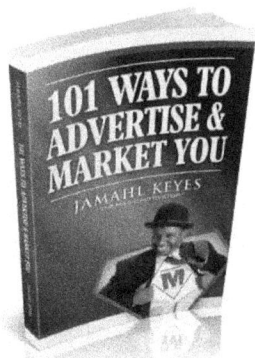

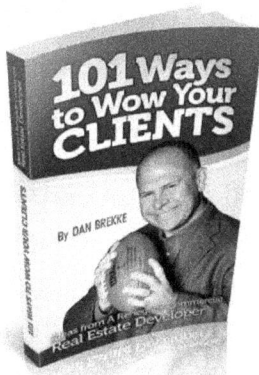

Putting Your Book to Work

Having a book is a great tool for acquiring new business.

But once you make the investment, you will probably find that it can do much more.

I have seen clients use their books to topple barriers and transform their businesses.

While many of the successes were to be expected, some were quite surprising. Just a couple of examples:

John Cannon.

John owns an auto repair shop in northern Indiana. He used his book successfully to grow his auto repair business. One of the members of a nominating committee found out about his new book and was so impressed he nominated John for the "businessman of the year" from the local chamber of commerce — and John won. John had been running his business for over 40 years and had never received such an honor. The exposure helped his business even more.

Dan Brekke.

Dan owns a manufacturing business. He provided his book as a resource for his business customers to use in building their businesses. When his customers do better, so does he.

Dan also had some real estate investments. When the real estate market tanked, he went through a period where he was "dirt rich but cash poor." At his annual review meeting with his bankers, they told him they would need to evaluate whether they could renew his operating loans for another year.

As the meeting ended, Dan handed a copy of his book to each banker. Suddenly the mood in the room shifted. They were impressed with his business acumen and how creative the book was. After a few minutes chatting about the book and hearing how it was benefiting his business, they decided to extend his operating loan.

I have heard story after story of how books have helped our clients transform their businesses. The exposure and credibility that these books can generate have resulted in a wide variety of opportunities — from invitations to public speaking events to joint venture business proposals to consulting engagements. The power of the books has opened doors our clients didn't even know existed.

One common occurrence is when a recipient of the book gives it to a friend or colleague to read.

> *"Here is the book my dentist, Dr. Jones, wrote on dental implants. I thought you might want to read about them as well."*

Now, your book becomes a great referral tool. This has a powerful ripple effect on your business.

One client I helped write his book owned a medical clinic. His book only took 20 minutes to read but helped the patients remember the details of the procedure and could also share it with their family and friends. In fact, the clinic would give the patient a second copy to pass on to their

friends. It became their #1 referral source –
which is why I call the books I write "lead
gen books."

Another effect of the book as a
business tool is the influence on profitability.
When your customer or prospect views you
as a trusted expert, they look at you as
someone who will solve their problems.
When they see you in this light, they tend to
be much less concerned with price as the
primary determinant of their purchase.

In some instances, you will even be
able to sell your goods or services at
premium prices due to your perceived
expertise!

**Client
Testimonials**

" — *Michael O'Dell*
CEO

We've done over 180 million dollars in
commisionable sales since Nina created
my magazine tear sheet . That magazine
is what put me on the map and is almost
exclusively responsible for my
exponential growth.

Why Does It Work?

The Celebrity Effect

In 1994, George Foreman began a second career as a paid endorser for the "lean mean grilling machine" that has become a worldwide retail success. Over 100 million George Foreman grills have been sold since that infomercial first hit TV.

Now, electric grills had been available from retailers for decades before George ever cooked a burger on one.

But until George said you should have one, very few people did.

This is the celebrity effect.

Our society really likes celebrities.

- We follow them,
- monitor their activities,
- and listen to their advice.

While you probably aren't going to be on the cover of Success Magazine as the result of your book's publication, you can leverage "celebrity" to some degree at the local level!

Renegade Business Success Magazine

Just because you won't be on the cover of Success Magazine, doesn't mean you can't be on ANY magazine.

I produce the Renegade Business Success Magazine where I put you on the cover and write a lead article all about you and talk about the principles in the book you just wrote.

You'll also be featured on RenegadeSpotlights.com. I call having a book the expert position and being on the cover of a magazine the celebrity affect.

Go to www.RenegadeBusinessSuccess.com to find out how you can be featured on the front of the magazine.

Press Releases

Using press releases, contacts with local media, and other methods of distribution, you can create a local "buzz" about your book. This not only impresses your existing customers; it can be a powerful driver for new business.

The "Expert Authority Phenomenon" Advantage

Now, let's discuss is the power of the "expert-authority-celebrity phenomenon."

When purchasing a product or service, most people will choose an expert over a novice.

Even a seller with a significantly lower price can easily be outsold based on the "expert-authority-celebrity phenomenon."

Not convinced?
Let's look at an example

You need brain surgery.

Do you go to the doctor right out of medical school who just opened his own practice?

Does his promise of a "half-price surgery" even make a dent in your decision?

Of course not. You want someone who is THE BEST.

Now, you may not be selling brain surgery, but that doesn't mean the same principles don't apply.

- What about your divorce lawyer?

- The company you hire to install your company's Internet security?

- Your hip replacement surgeon?

- Your appliance repair person?

ALL businesses can benefit from the expert authority phenomenon. Take a roofer, for example. You may think as long as the new roofing is comparable, most people will choose the lowest price. Well, not always.

If your book explains the difference between using a cut rate, fly-by-night contractor versus a well-established reputable contractor – the one who wrote the book on roofing – you have a greater chance of getting the job.

At this point you may be thinking, "I am a good (roofer, dentist, insurance agent), but I am no expert."

I understand that. Believe me...even though I've been doing marketing for 25 years, written some million-dollar sales letters, and am known all around the world for my direct mail piece that looks like a man's paper wallet (www.Wallet-Mailer.com), I guarantee you there is someone out there better than me, more qualified, more credentialed.

But they haven't written the book of marketing ideas. Nor do they have 10 books on Amazon like I do.

Writing a book takes you into a category of one.

You just have to use that power.

Perception Is Everything

Let's say your air conditioner breaks down in the middle of the summer. You call a repair company.

They let you know that their technician will be bringing a trainee along on the appointment.

A couple of hours later, the technician arrives at the door. Next to him is a long-haired kid about 20 years old. You think he looks like someone who would be better suited to delivering pizzas.

You tell the tech how nice it is that he is showing this new guy the ropes. Just then the kid says, "*Actually, I am training him.*"

Just because of appearances, you assumed the older man was the experienced tech. You hadn't even considered the kid had been working alongside his father in this business since he was old enough to carry a wrench.

My point is, **perception is EVERYTHING.** You see most people have NO IDEA what a good person in your field looks like. They don't know, and if you do your job right, they will never experience what your competition is like.

If your divorce lawyer gets you the outcome you desire, is it even possible (should you need one again) you would use anyone else?

If your friend asks you for a referral, would you recommend anyone else? NO. If you do a great job, your customers will do the same.

You don't need to BE the best—just perceived as the best.

Your book (and cover of the magazine) will help build that perception for you!

When deciding who to hire...

Nothing is more expensive than a cheap price.

Nothing cheaper than an expensive price.

4

What Should Your Book Be About?

B y now, I hope I've convinced you that you need to write a book!

You have realized the benefits of a book and are now ready to begin the steps to get yours done.

There are several types of books. Each one has specific benefits that work well to accomplish certain goals. Knowing what you want to accomplish and how you are going to use your book, will affect what your book should be about.

No matter what type of book you choose, though, it should always start with your story.

Book Type 1: Detailed Information on a Specific Topic

This type of book works great when your goal is to simply establish yourself as "the authority" in a particular industry.

I've licensed the content and produced this type of book to insurance agents, cosmetic surgeons, financial planners, realtors, dentists, orthopaedic surgeons and more.

For Insurance Agents

Consumers buy car insurance, homeowner's insurance, or liability insurance because they know they have the possibility of loss in those areas. Our book outlines 20 additional places that you may incur a loss should certain conditions apply to you. The book actually provokes concern in the reader's mind. It makes the reader more aware of potential losses.

Not only that – there's a whole section on commercial insurance so it's target market is focused on business owners who need both personal and commercial insurance PLUS have employees that also need insurance. Are you getting the idea?

The reason the book works so well is that it's not SELLING more insurance. It's EDUCATING your reader about additional areas of exposure without coming off as a hard-sell salesperson.

People like to buy – they don't like to be sold.

Your job is to educate them which is what I do when I write the draft of your lead generating book for you to fine tuen.

Book Type 2: Information on a General Topic

Sometimes it can be better to write a book on a general interest topic rather than specific products or services.

For example, in businesses such as financial services, it can be difficult to get a book about investing approved by compliance. So a book of general interest geared to your ideal prospect can work in your favor

One book that works well for financial planners is our bucket list book.

This book is not about how to get more money, but what to do with the money that your investments will yield. The book paints a picture of a meaningful and exciting future using the money you will make.

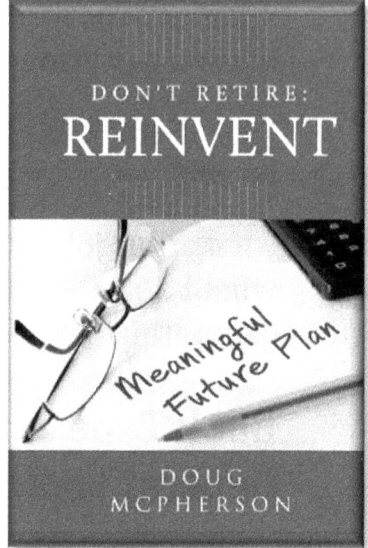

Here's an example of one of the books I helped a financial planner write.

If you are helping your clients create a nest egg for their future, a book on how to make that future more rewarding will be seen as a very helpful item.

A number of our clients use my *101 Marketing Ideas* book I spoke about in chapter 2. This has been published as "The Wow Effect," "101 Ways to Wow Your Clients," and various other titles. If your company markets business-to-business (B to B), your target prospect is a business owner.

This book tells your prospects how to market and build their business more effectively. And when they are doing well, your business will likewise improve.

Remember, you are trying to use the book as a way to initiate or build a relationship with a client, customer, or patient. In many cases that relationship is more vital to your business than almost all other factors in your enterprise.

Book Type 3: The Fun or Entertaining Book

Some of my clients like to start with a book that is just fun and interesting, with little to no overall emphasis on "hard facts" about the business per se.

A book of funny quips, one-liners, or interesting quotes is one sometimes called a "coaster book" or "end-table book." It is usually one that can be read very quickly or can be scanned and read a few pages at a time.

Many times, these are the kinds of books you see in waiting rooms, casual meeting areas, or on your end table at home.

While these books are not focused on your company or industry like some of our other books, they are quick to assemble and will allow you to be up and running even faster.

Book Type 4: The Sales Letter Book

This one is the most powerful and the most effective type of books I help clients write.

24-**HOUR** Salesperson

I call it a 24 hour salesperson. It's job is do 90% of the selling for you.

It is also the most difficult to do and get right.

A sales letter book is exactly what it sounds like. It is a well written sales letter compiled in book form, designed to sell you and what you do to your prospect.

Along the way you are educating and sharing information.

Ideally a book could lead a prospect into a

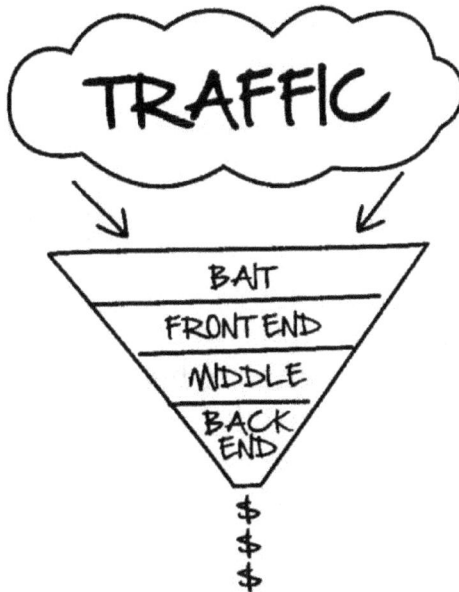

"nurture funnel" where you can keep the relationship going.

Russell Brunson is a brilliant direct response marketer who perfected the sales book funnel. He uses the book as "the bait" as shown in this diagram.

According to Brunson, there are 7 main phases of the buyers journey through the sales funnel:

1. Awareness - This is the top of the funnel where you make potential customers aware of your product/service. This usually involves things like social media, , in-person marketing, content marketing, ads, etc. to drive traffic.

2. Interest - Next you spark their interest and get them engaged with things like an opt-in page with a lead magnet (your book).

3. Consideration - Here you provide valuable information to help them consider if your product or service is right for them. This is where you educate them. If they got your book by downloading it online, your continue to nurture the relationship through things like email sequences, webinars, product demos, etc.

4. Decision - Now you give them an offer and opportunity to decide if they want to purchase. This can (but not always) involve some kind of low-priced introductory offer. Of course the offer depends on your product/service. Orthopaedic surgeons can't offer a trial hip replacement.

5. Onboarding - After they purchase, you onboard them as a customer and help them get set up and achieve success quickly. Welcome emails, orientation calls, support resources, shock and awe boxes (also known as trust boxes).

6. Ascension - Look for opportunities to provide more value, additional products/services, higher levels of your core offer, etc. to help them ascend to being a raving fan.

7. Loyalty - Turn satisfied repeat customers into loyal brand advocates who refer others. Things like loyalty programs, incentives, community.

The goal is to move leads step-by-step through each phase, customizing messaging and offers based on where they are in their buyer journey.

Here's a picture of what the buyers journey looks like

THE 7 PHASES OF A FUNNEL

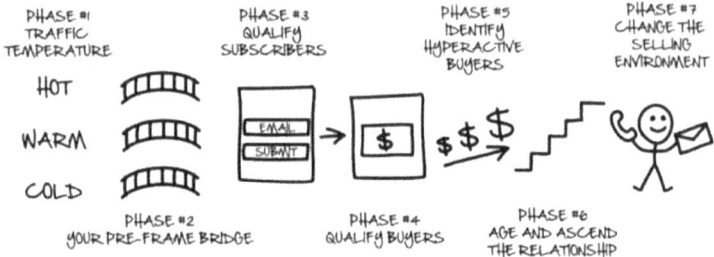

PHASE #1
TRAFFIC
TEMPERATURE

HOT
WARM
COLD

PHASE #3
QUALIFY
SUBSCRIBERS

EMAIL
SUBMIT

PHASE #5
IDENTIFY
HYPERACTIVE
BUYERS

$

$ $ $

PHASE #7
CHANGE THE
SELLING
ENVIRONMENT

PHASE #2
YOUR PRE-FRAME BRIDGE

PHASE #4
QUALIFY BUYERS

PHASE #6
AGE AND ASCEND
THE RELATIONSHIP

A good sales letter book is very conversational; it follows the same processes and models as a good marketing piece (PAS, or Problem – Agitate – Solve).

If you have already developed a great sales letter or webinar for your business, many times you can use that as a good source around which to begin and build a book.

Your sales letter book can become THE BEST lead magnet into your buyers journey funnel

Book Type 5: The Testimonial Book

This type of book is a collection of testimonials from your customers, clients or patients. This book is ideal as an additional tool in your arsenal. It can be effective as your only book, but it really has a different objective and works in different ways than the other book types outlined here.

Here's an example of one I did for a weight loss surgeon. It is a way in print to show overwhelming "social proof" that you do what you say you will do. It functions much like online reviews that companies post on their websites.

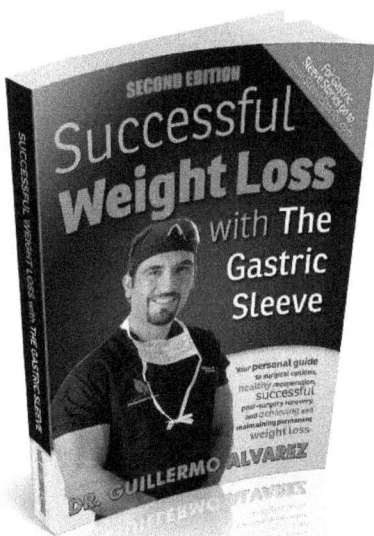

Your lead gen book builds the perception that you are a really good (fill in the blank).

A testimonial book proves it by presenting stories and comments from people who actually tried your services.

Combining these two types of books with a book funnel AND as part of a shock and awe box can catapult your business on autopilot.

**To see how I used both of these books in this client's
shock and awe box, go to
www.ShockAndAweBoxIdea.com.**

Book Type 6: The Sales Letter and Testimonial Combination Book

This is THE best book for business owners. Here's a perfect example of a combination book I helped Claude write. If you want to see it go to **ClaudesBook.com**.

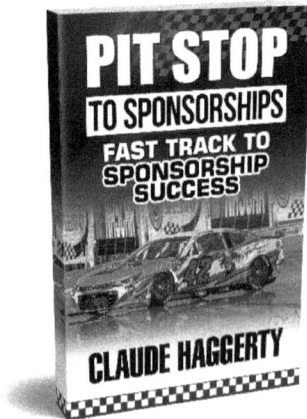

— Billy Wagner
CEO - Brightway Insurance

INSURANCE
TIMES TODAY

"I put Nina in charge of finishing my book and she got it done and shipped to me in under sixty days. That was an amazing accomplishment. It's completely first class.

Getting Your Book DONE

But I am NOT a writer!

N ow you have made the decision to write a book. And you know what kind of book you want to write.

The next step is to GET IT DONE.

This is the step where most people freeze.

They panic.

"I am NOT a writer," they protest. "How will I ever have a book?"

Having a book with YOUR cover and YOUR name on it is much easier than you think. AnThere are six main ways to accomplish the task. Each one has its cost in time and money.

Here are your choices.

1. You can write the book yourself
2. You can hire a ghost writer
3. You can hire am author's coach
4. You can license your book content
5. You can be part of a multi author book
6. You can hire a marketing company (like us) who understand how to help you write books that sell and become your 24 hour salesperson.

1. Write the Book Yourself

Writing a book is a daunting task. Many books are started and never finished. Many have never even been started. Although writing your own book bears the least out-of-pocket cost, the cost in time and effort can be immense. In writing a book there are so many questions:

- How do I write something that isn't boring?
- How do I write something that properly tells the story I want to tell?

- How do I write it so that my customers will be compelled to buy, and buy from me?

While 80 percent of people will probably never read your book, the 20 percent who do will know if you know your stuff and make their decision to purchase based on your words.

As if that's not pressure enough, then even more questions arise:
- Who will edit it?
- How do I get my cover designed?
- How do I publish it?
- What's an ISBN number?
- How do I get printed copies?

Resources do exist now to help you with parts of this— but you can see it is a large task to make happen in a timely manner – particularly if you've never written AND published a book. (don't forget writing a book is only one part of the equation).

Pros:
- Low financial investment.

Cons:
- Massive investment in time.
- Need to learn how to "sell in print."
- Have to learn all the book publishing details and find designers and editors.

Conclusion: For most business owners, this is not a viable option.

2. Hire a Ghost Writer

Many celebrities that publish a book don't actually do the writing. A ghost writer interviews them, develops the concepts for the book and gets paid a hefty fee to write a book in the voice of the "author" of the book.

Selecting a ghost writer is the most important task in this case. You need to hire someone who can convey the essence of your sales message though the words in your book. This is a tough task for many ghost writers.

Cost can often come into play in this case. I know one writer who charges $150,000. Another well-known book publisher charges $50,000 and another person who only coaches you to write yourself charges $30,000.

Just like anything, you get what you pay for.

Pros:
- You don't need to spend every waking hour working on your book.
- Your significant other will remember what you look like.

Cons:
- Large investment.
- No guarantee you will have a "salesman in print."
- You still have to get it published

Conclusion: While this is a way to get a book done, it can be costly and results are not guaranteed.

3. Hire an Author's Coach

An author's coach typically provides a range of services to help writers improve their craft and achieve their writing goals.

They do NOT write the book for you but help create an outline and give constructive feedback as needed.

They also can keep you focused on a timeline and goal to get your book finished.

Most of the time they do NOT publish your book but may recommend publishers for you to use.

Pros:
- You can have an objective perspective on your writing
- With their guidance you should be able to accelerate your writing

Cons:
- Large investment. I've seen coaches charge as much as $30,000 to coach (not write)
- No guarantee you will have a "salesman in print." They focus more on story style writing.
- You still have to figure out how to get it published. I've seen example after example of manuscripts still in the computer the never get in a printed/published form.

Conclusion: While this is a way to get a book done, it can be costly and results for using as a sales tool are not guaranteed.

4. Use Licensed Book Content

Licensing content already written is the easiest and quickest way to become a published author. The book cannot be put on Amazon but it can become your lead magnet in your book funnel, your 24 hour salesperson and give you that critical expert status.

With licensed content you don't own the copyrights. I retain those, but I customize the cover and title so no one knows it wasn't 100% original content.

When you license book content from me, I also give you the right to do a bit of fine tuning of the content to make it more what you want it to say.

You have your own custom cover, and have the ability to revise any of the content inside the book, but it is essentially the same book.

You don't own the copyrights to the content – but you do license the rights to use the book to create expert status in a specific geographical area.

For example, if you are a dentist, this is a 3- to 5-mile radius from your patients' homes.

So a dentist from Dayton, Ohio, and one from Phoenix, Arizona, can have essentially the same content in their book. But because the titles, covers, and authors of the book are different, no one will ever know.

Here are three examples of covers of a book we did on insurance. All of these books have basically the same inside contents. But they look different, have different titles and "different" authors.

The same thing applies, with a slight variation, to targeting a specific niche.

For example, you sell after-market parts to John Deere tractor owners. If someone else targets owners of Case-International tractors, there's little, if any, overlap.

Pros:
- You don't need to be spending every waking hour working on your book.
- Your book will be a tested, proven lead generating salesperson.
- You can have copies of your new book FAST.
- It's a cost-effective way to get a book done quickly.
- You can edit it any way you want and are not starting with a blank screen to write.

Cons:
- It won't be on Amazon or Kindle
- We can't take you to Amazon Best Seller status

Conclusion: For most business owners, this is the best option. Your prospects will see you as the go-to expert authority who will help them solve their problem.

5. Be part of a multi-author book

If you don't have time to write your own book, but you want to have the bragging rights to becoming an amazon Best Seller, this option might be perfect for you.

Being part of 5-10 other authors in a single book is the least expensive way to have your name on a book and the authority that comes with that.

Pros:
- You don't need to be spending every waking hour working on your book.
- It will be on Amazon and Kindle.
- We can take the book to an Amazon Best Seller status.
- Your picture can be on the back cover of the book.
- We do the writing for you.
- It's the least expensive way to become an author.

Cons:
- You share the "author" title with other contributors.

Conclusion: This is a great option. Your prospects will see you as the go-to expert authority who will help them solve their problem.

6. Hire a Marketing Company who specializes in custom-written lead generating-books

If your book is not a legacy book – or one where you tell your life's story – then you need to hire a marketing company who specializes in writing what I call "a long-form sales letter book"..

It will become your 24 hr salesperson

It's going to do all the cold calling and will work 365 days a year/24 hours a day without taking time off.

That's a lot to ask of a book. It must be written with the end goal in mind and a call to action at the end.

It does take a special writer to do this.

Most ad agencies and marketing companies get paid for creating "pretty" things that dazzle the owner much more than the target customer, so choosing the right company here is VITAL.

This is mostly "sales in print," meaning you are making each book your marketing soldier.

You want each soldier outfitted with the best weapons possible, armed with tactics and strategies that will all but guarantee success.

If you want killer soldiers, you don't send them to beauty school. You send them to Navy SEAL training camp!

Pros:
- Your book is focused EXACTLY on your specialty or niche.
- Your significant other will remember what you look like.
- It can become an Amazon Best Seller (that's a HUGE benefit that is often worth the investment) so you can now be introduced as an Amazon best selling author.
- You can repurpose all the content in other ways to market your business.

Cons:

- You may need to provide a lot of source info. This is made better if you have many audios, videos, blog posts, or marketing materials to base your book on. Or if you hire us to write the book we'll conduct interviews with you and have them transcribed.
- Hiring an agency to do a custom book for you is also expensive.

Conclusion: This is a good way to get a custom book written., become a best-selling author and own the rights to the content to repurpose in your marketing.

Client Testimonial

— *Bert Molner*
CEO - Treefrog Photography

Nina had my book written, edited, formatted, cover artwork done, biography and foreword all done within a matter of weeks, and at a small fraction of what my friend had invested to do his own book. To my surprise, it was the best business card I could have imagined.

6

OK, Got My Book— NOW WHAT?

Put your 24 hour salesperson to work!

First, you must understand you cannot use your book as a lead generating machine if your books—your "salespeople"— are in still in the box.

By now I've at least got you thinking that "maybe" writing a book to show your expertise would help you sell more and become more profitable.

You've decided what kind of book you want help getting done first and we've got the book finished and published.

The box has arrived to your office.

It's time to open the box and put them to work.

When deploying them, keep this overall strategy in mind.

You want to get your book into the hands of as many qualified prospects as possible

Here are five strategies to getting your lead generating book working for you.

Cinch the Deal

If you provide bids, proposals, or quotes, include a copy of your book along with your bids. Go out of your way to point it out. "Oh, by the way, I have included a copy of my new book, and I have autographed it for you." Many times you will close your deal based just on this easy statement.

Send the book before the appointment

If your client/patient is visiting your professional practice for a "free consultation," have your staff ask if they could mail a copy of the book before them come in to see you. By the time they arrive they will have spent the 20-30 minutes to read the book and have begun to know, like and trust you.

As a bonus, be sure to autograph the book before your staff sends it out.

Trade Shows and Networking Events

When you truly understand your book is your 24 hour salesperson, you'll realize the more you have them out their working, the more sales – and profit – you'll make.

You may think that just giving them away to everyone gets your name out there faster, but we've found that isn't really the case. Just leaving them to take at a trade show or networking event doesn't work.

Instead, offer to autograph your book, ask their name. Make it personal. (That's another good way to make sure it stays on their shelf forever!)

Get Media Attention

When you get your books, do some research on your local media. Find out who at your local TV, radio, and newspaper does stories on your business. Take the time to create a press release, and mail it along with a copy of your book to your local media outlets. Local media are always looking for stories of local interest.

You may or may not get a story right away, but often when a situation arises concerning the area of expertise in your book, they will look you up.

Here's 30 ideas for media exposure.

1. Announce an upcoming book launch or release

2. Share an intriguing or controversial excerpt from your book

3. Release new research or statistics related to your book's topic

4. Comment on a current event tied to your area of expertise

5. Reveal the biggest myth or misconception related to your book's subject

6. Offer a list of tips or advice from your book

7. Create an info-graphic or quiz based on your book

8. Share celebrity or expert endorsements for your book

9. Announce you're hosting a book signing or speaking event

10. Get certified or accredited related to your book's focus

11. Start an awareness day, contest, or online campaign around your book's theme

12. Share your personal story or experience that inspired writing the book

13. Use holidays or cultural events to connect with your book's subject

14. Announce an online course, webinar, or training program aligned to your book

15. Offer controversial predictions or forecasts related to your area of study

16. Announce a charity partnership, cause campaign, or donation around your book's message

17. Conduct or reference a survey, poll or new research supporting your book

18. Create an interesting list or comparison, such as "5 Common Myths vs. Facts"

19. Offer your hot take or insight on the latest related news story

20. Announce a book giveaway promotion

21. Share what inspired your interest and passion for this book's topic

22. Discuss who would most benefit from reading your book

23. Reveal what sets your book apart from others in the genre

24. Announce you surpassed a book sales milestone

25. Discuss dramatic moments or surprises people will read about

26. Announce a book-inspired documentary, movie deal, or television appearance

27. Provide a reading recommendation list of similar books

28. Share your pet peeves related to misinformation on this book's topic

29. Provide your outlook on the future or projections related to this subject area

30. Offer counterintuitive advice that goes against mainstream recommendations.

Keep sending nationally syndicated press releases every week or every other week and always refer back to your book. Guaranteed the media will soon be calling you as the subject matter expert in your field.

Nationally Syndicated Press Releases

One of my insurance agent clients from Canada, Greg Marcyniuk, took the initiative and did just that. After a particularly bad winter, the spring thaw resulted in a large problem with flooding. Two of his local media called him, wanting his perspective on the issue from an insurance company's point of view. This book got him local publicity for free!

Supply copies of your book to your referral partners

Now for the truly AWESOME way to use your book that will really make your competition scratch their heads.

Referral partners are often the best place to get quality leads. Even if you don't already have a referral situation, you can almost instantly gain one using this strategy.

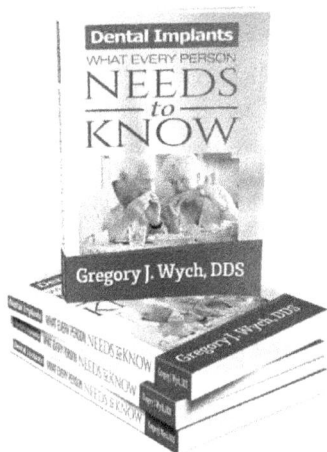

Let's say you are an dental implant specialist. You get many of your new patients from general practice dentists. So, send a few copies of your book, *What Every Person Needs to Know About Implants* to dentists with whom you'd like to share referrals. Just simply ask them to offer a copy of that book to ANYONE who needs more information about implants. That's all there is to it. Send ten copies of the book and just wait.

If you start asking your new patients, you will quickly hear, Dr. Jones, gave me a copy of your book." BINGO!

To keep this train cranking right along, on a monthly schedule, call your referral partners and ask if they still have copies or if they need more of them. Keeping your partners' offices fully stocked with your books will only bring in more and more new patients.

Now, I know you are saying, "I don't have an easy referral partner like that. Who can I use?" Here is the test to decide if the business would be a good partner.

1. They have a relationship with your ideal customer.
2. They can offer "extra" to those people by providing free information that would make them look good.

3. You solve a problem for them.

Here are a few examples of potentially good partnerships:

- Cosmetic Surgeon/Hair Salon/Spa
- Roofing Contractor/Lumberyard
- Divorce Lawyer/Couples' therapists
- Realtor/Mortgage broker
- Implant specialist/General dentist

That's Not All!

Becoming an author is **step 1**.

Becoming an Amazon Best Selling Author is **step 2**.

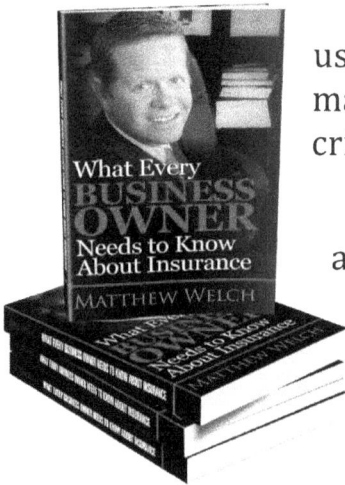

Getting and using your book marketing assets is a critical **step 3**.

We also give our authors 3D version of their book covers to use in their marketing and social media.

When we work with our new "authors" we also give them a special report with 41 ways to use their books to make money in their business.

Ideas like:

1. Send a free copy to your email list and ask them to share with friends if they like it.

2. Bring copies to networking events and conferences to hand out.

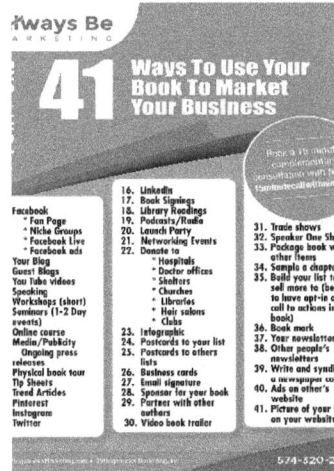

Always Be MARKETING

41 Ways To Use Your Book To Market Your Business

Facebook
* Fan Page
^ Niche Groups
* Facebook Live
* Facebook ads
Your Blog
Guest Blogs
You Tube videos
Speaking
Workshops (short)
Seminars (1-2 Day events)
Online course
Media/Publicity
Ongoing press releases
Physical book tour
Tip Sheets
Treed Articles
Pinterest
Instagram
Twitter

16. LinkedIn
17. Book Signings
18. Library Readings
19. Podcasts/Radio
20. Launch Party
21. Networking Events
22. Donate to
* Hospitals
* Doctor offices
* Shelters
* Churches
* Libraries
* Hair salons
* Clubs
23. Infographic
24. Postcards to your list
25. Postcards to others lists
26. Business cards
27. Email signature
28. Sponsor for your book
29. Partner with other authors
30. Video book trailer

31. Trade shows
32. Speaker One Sh
33. Package book w other items
34. Sample a chapter
35. Build your list to sell more to (be to have opt-in o call to actions in book)
36. Book mark
37. Your newsletter
38. Other people's newsletters
39. Write and syndi a newspaper col
40. Ads on other's website
41. Picture of your on your websit

574-520-2

3. Use your book as a lead magnet on your website and put them into a nurture funnel.

4. Mail out copies to targeted prospects with a personalized note.

5. Run advertisements with a free copy of your book as the offer (i.e. send them to your book funnel website).

6. Guest post on relevant blogs and offer the book as a download.

7.   Hold book signings at bookstores.

8.   Send review copies to bloggers and influencers in your industry.

9.   Give away free copies at speaking engagements.

10.   Partner with other businesses to bundle your book as a free bonus.

11.   Promote excerpts on social media.

12.   Run Facebook and Instagram ads driving to the free download page.

13.   Add a QR code on all marketing materials that goes to the book's site.

14.   Allow free previews of sample chapters online.

15.   Give copies to charity auction winners.

16.   Send copies to prospects when doing cold outreach.

17.   Run Amazon Kindle promotions with temporary price reductions.

Our most successful business authors join our authors mastermind where we brainstorm and hold owners accountable for getting their books working for them.

We also

- Send out press releases to get members mentioned in national news publications.
- Interview them for our nationally syndicated podcast..
- Feature them on the front cover of the Renegade Business success Magazine.

Client Testimonial

— Jerry Jones
Jerry Jones Direct

"(a book) can really **change the way your practice is viewed** in your community. You can easily go from someone who is invisible to everyone, just another dentist in the crowd, to someone who rises up and is seen.

It is amazing what a book can do to **elevate your authority, your credibility, and your status** among the community.

A book is much easier than you think, Megabucks Marketing is THE folks you want to see when you want to get your book done.

It's **super simple, super effective** an will literally change the way everyone in your community sees you.

The minute you get your book going, get it started, get it done, and put it to use, you will **wonder why you didn't do it ten years earlier.**"

TAKE ACTION

Bottom line? You're losing—yes, LOSING—money every day you don't have a book. You are losing money with every prospect who would have bought from you if they'd had a copy of your book proving you are the best solution for their problem.

- YES, you will need to make an investment.
- YES, this concept might be new to you.
- YES, it will mean a change in the way you do business.

But, what is your alternative? You can continue doing what you have always done. You can wait for the phone to ring. You can chase people and beg them to buy from you. You can continue to watch your competitors eating up more and more of your market share.

When we put it that way, "same-old" doesn't sound like such a good choice, does it?

You have been looking for a way to finally transform your business and give you the advantage you've been looking for.

THIS IS THAT ADVANTAGE!

Look, I know making changes can be scary.

I know you have invested in marketing before that have not worked.

I can assure you this is not another fancy "gadget" that will be outdated in 6 months. I don't care if you sell marbles or perform brain surgery, I know it will work in your business.

My goal here is for you to take back your business and start making the kind of money you need to not only survive but prosper! It is local businesses like you that are the backbone of this nation. When our small businesses are strong, our nation is strong.

Conclusion

So, the decision is yours. What will it be? Are you willing to accept your current status quo, or do you want to really pour on the gas and take your market by storm? I have a quote on my wall; I am reading it now. It says:

If it is important, you will find a way; if not, you will find an excuse.

So, what's it going to be? Another excuse, or a better way?

To get started now, schedule a free call with me to talk about your particular situation. Go to

www.CallWithNina.com

Client Testimonial

" — *Dr. Kenneth Vinton*

Nina, I have to say we love, love, love, the book! We can directly track nearly a quarter of a million dollars in increase sales to the use of the book In the past 6 or 7 months. It informs the reader as to what we do, positions us as an expert, and all but eliminates recommendation and price resistance. I should have done this years ago. Thank you!

Appendix A
License Book Examples

Here are some books we currently have available for licensing, and who uses them to grow their businesses. We're adding books all the time so if you don't see yours, call and ask if we have it.

INSURANCE BOOK

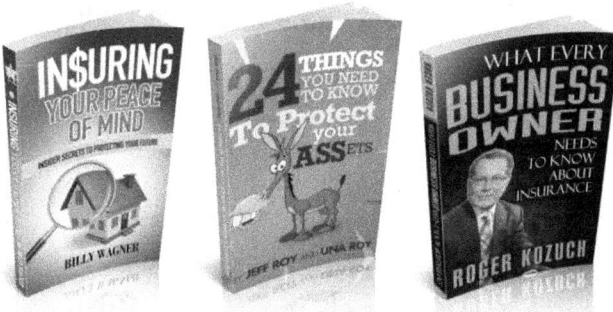

Any independent agent who is finding their business being destroyed by the online "big guys" can use a book to get customers who no longer even care about "saving 15 percent in 15 minutes or less." Use your book to target lucrative niches, increase add-on policies, and open doors to clients who seem to be focused on saving a buck instead of having peace of mind.

We have this book available for your agency if you live in the USA or Canada. Both versions explain in detail the rules and regulations of coverage, as well as the benefits of KNOWING you are protected.

Well suited for:
- Insurance Agents / Brokers

GENERAL DENISTRY BOOK

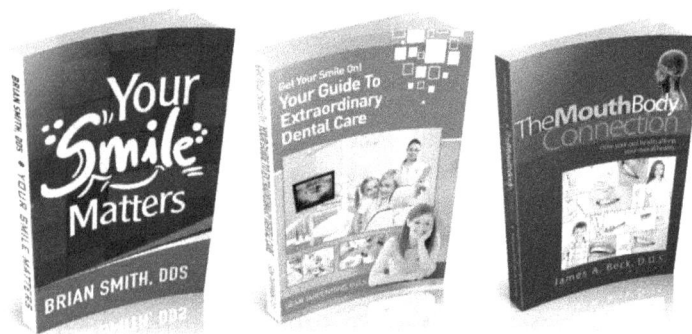

Dentists these days find themselves fighting a tough battle. With stiff competition, the rising cost of health care, and the growth of corporate dentistry, dentists are looking for a way to stand out.

This book answers the big questions in any patient's mind about dental care.

One exciting trend in dentistry today is the additional services now available at your local dentist. From implants to "smile makeovers," Botox® treatments or help for sleep apnea, the services your local dental office can provide go far beyond just cleanings and crowns.

Well suited for:
- General Dentists
- Orthodontists
- Pediatric Dentists
- Periodontists

DENTAL IMPLANT BOOK

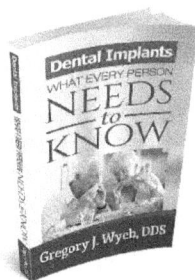

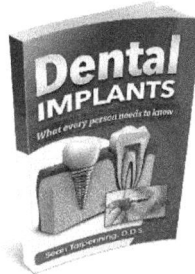

This is a 24-hour implant salesman book. If one case is worth at least $5,000 this is a MUST book for all implant dentists.

BUCKET LIST BOOK

Our bucket list book is a great door-opener for you if you are in the financial world—if you sell business opportunities or deal in wealth-building or retention products or services. This is a great book for you if you help enable a lifestyle of prosperity and success.

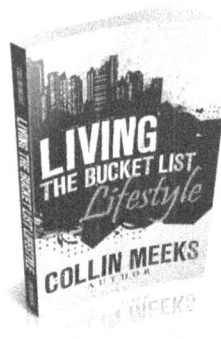

Well suited for:
- Financial Planners
- Lifestyle coaches/Consultants
- Investment/Income Strategy Businesses

"101 WAYS" MARKETING BOOK

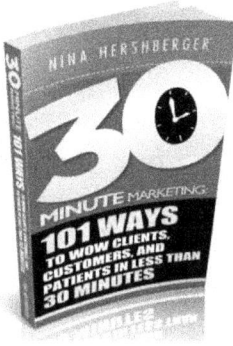

Marketing is the universal business language. If you sell ANYTHING B2B, you need to offer your customers your book on how to market themselves. When you help them improve their business, you are seen as a partner in the journey, NOT an adversary.

Well suited for:
- Manufacturers
- Wholesalers
- Marketing Companies
- Coaches/Consultants
- Advertising Agencies

CLIENTS FOR LIFE

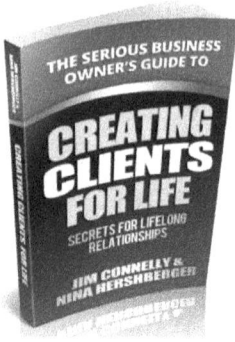

Great customer relationships are one of the biggest factors that create real value in your business. Providing a book that helps your business customers build better relationships with their customers will make you look like a hero.

Well suited for:
- Manufacturers
- Wholesalers
- Marketing Companies
- Coaches/Consultants
- Advertising Agencies
- Contractors
- Any business selling to consumers

CUSTOM WRITTEN BOOKS AND HOW THEY WERE USED IN THESE "ORDINARY" BUSINESSES

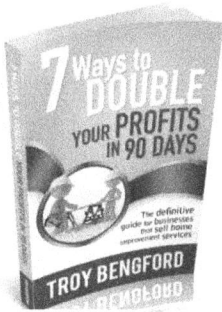

Marketing Ideas book used to generate leads for a coaching and consulting client who provides home services.

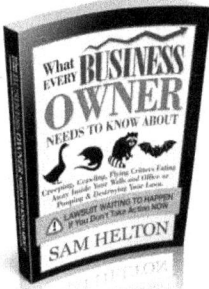

Lead generation book for a client who traps wild animals and repairs damage made by them in homes and businesses. We actually wrote two versions, one for residential and one for business customers.

This client provides exit strategy planning. He also has created a system to "reinvent, not retire" business owners who exit their businesses.

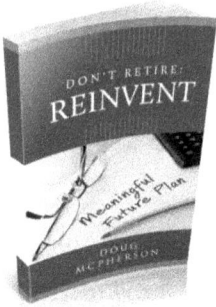

This book is used to provide quality information on let your agency fall the online guys. how to not insurance victim to He uses this book to get new prospects to join his coaching group.

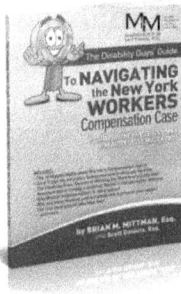

Using these "mini" books, this lawyer provides valuable information to his prospective clients. They have ordered and given out hundreds of these books.

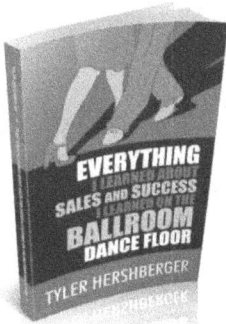

Do you have an unusual passion? This client created a fun, short and simple book how he related his ballroom dance experience to selling.

Sometimes you don't the story. testimonials story for killer way to your new

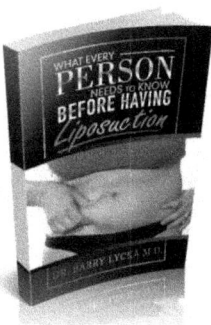

need to tell Using your to tell your you can be a introduce company to prospects.

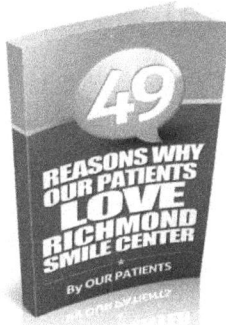

The most lucrative procedure for a cosmetic surgeon is liposuction. Booking one or two more lipo patients can pay off your investment.

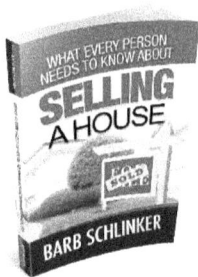

REAL ESTATE

Used as part of your listing process these books will put you in a league of your own. You're the realtor who wrote the book on buying and selling a house.

Let's Get Started!

www.CallWithNina.com

Nina Hershberger, CEO
Megabucks Marketing, Inc.
574-320-2522
Nina@megabucksmarketing.com

www.ingramcontent.com/pod-product-compliance
Lightning Source LLC
Chambersburg PA
CBHW070944210326
41520CB00021B/7044